The leading organisation for professional management

As the champion of management, the Chartered Management Institute shapes and supports the managers of tomorrow. By sharing intelligent insights and setting standards in management development, the Institute helps to deliver results in a dynamic world.

Setting and raising standards

The Institute is a nationally accredited organisation, responsible for setting standards in management and recognising excellence through the award of professional qualifications.

Encouraging development, improving performance

The Institute has a vast range of development programmes, qualifications, information resources and career guidance to help managers and their organisations meet new challenges in a fast-changing environment.

Shaping opinion

With in-depth research and regular policy surveys of its 91,000 individual members and 520 corporate members, the Chartered Management Institute has a deep understanding of the key issues. Its view is informed, intelligent and respected.

For more information call 01536 204222 or visit www.managers.org.uk

C O N T E N T S

■ I N T R O D U C T I O N ■

Why do we need a book about customer care? After all, top management in many companies have always been telling everyone, and particularly their customers and staff, that customer satisfaction is the company's prime aim.

In many instances that was all that top management did about it – talk. More and more companies now realise that positive action is required to ensure that words do not remain mere platitudes. Often, management actions and attitudes contradict the stated intent to regard customer satisfaction as their highest priority.

After reading this book we will better understand:

- What customer care is and its effect on profits
- The role of the first-line manager in customer care
- The meaning of customer care and its use as a competitive tool
- The elements influencing customer care
- Ways of enhancing customer relations
- The importance of communication
- How to turn a complaint into a positive experience
- Why involvement of all staff is essential
- The need for setting standards and monitoring results
- Some management tools and aids available
- How to develop and implement a customer care programme
- Ways of building on past successes

Customer care in general

Today we will deepen our understanding of:

- What customer care is
- The value added by customer care
- The reason for its growing importance
- The role of the first-line manager

The quality of the product or service (for brevity's sake, please assume I mean 'product or service' when I write 'product' in the rest of this book) is a prerequisite for fighting the competitive battle in the market-place. Customers are entitled to presume that the product they intend to purchase is of a high quality, and they will make their purchasing decisions based on a much wider range of requirements. The companies which will be able to satisfy the largest number of these needs will be the winners in the long term.

We will examine a little later how we can establish what customers really expect from us as suppliers. What we must be convinced of is that satisfying these needs as fully as possible will make our products more desirable in the eyes of the customer, make him buy more or pay a premium for this benefit, and this in turn will improve our long-term success.

This customer care (or support) adds to the perceived value of our product and will encourage customers to come back to our company when they either need to replace it or when they need another product in our range.

Tom Peters put it extremely succinctly when he wrote, 'The essence of excellence is the thousand concrete, minute actions performed by everyone in an organisation to keep a company on course.' (*In Search of Excellence* (1982) T. J. Peters and R. H. Waterman, Harper and Row.)

What is customer care?

Before we examine this question let us identify the purpose of our business. The immediate conclusion will be that 'profit' must be the aim of all companies, because without profit, a business cannot survive in the longer term. We need to look into this simple statement a little more deeply.

What enables our company to make a profit? First, it needs to satisfy customer needs at a price the customer is willing and able to pay. Second, the supplier must be able to make or procure the product or service at a cost which, after adding overheads, still falls sufficiently far below the price that can be charged to customers to allow a reasonable profit margin. Thus our company can work on:

a making the total product offered to the customer more
   attractive
b reducing the cost of the product and/or of the
   company's overheads
c reducing its profit margin

Obviously, the most attractive option is to make the total
product offering as attractive as possible to the customer to
warrant charging a higher price. This, of course, does not
preclude working as efficiently as possible to reduce costs or
considering lower margins to attract more sales. These latter
options tend to be more painful, as reducing costs may have
adverse effects on customer support or product quality and
lower profit margins will affect shareholders' satisfaction
and financial market valuations.

Although these facts have been recognised, many
companies concentrate exclusively on cost reductions.

We can see that value to the customer can be added by non-
product activities. These activities can take many forms. For
instance, more helpful counter clerks at an airline check-in
counter, improved layout and signposting in a supermarket,
a more customer-orientated queuing system in a bank or
post office, easier telephone access to individual
departments, more thoughtful parking arrangements for
customers, etc. If we really give this matter some thought,
all of us can find ways of improving how we, as customers,
would like to be dealt with. If we really think about our
company's working procedures, there will be many
activities that each one of us can identify that would
enhance our support to customers.

So let us come back to 'What is customer care?' It consists of a variety of tangible and intangible elements.

Tangible elements
These are factors which can be seen or felt, heard or tasted. Many of these factors can be measured relatively easily. They are often based on skills which can be taught and learned. Examples of tangible elements include aspects such as product features (e.g. size, weight, colour, etc.) speed, ease of access, etc.

Intangible elements
These are much more difficult to define. They are also more difficult to measure and are often more subjective. They are highly dependent on attitudes which can be influenced but not taught. Examples of intangible elements include making the customer feel secure, relaxed, trusting, and well disposed towards the supplier and the individual members of staff.

As customer care consists of both these elements, it is our responsibility as managers to ensure that:

- The relevant skills are available by either recruiting staff who have already acquired these skills or by ensuring that these skills are imparted to existing or new staff by training, example, and leadership
- The right environment exists or is created to influence the attitude of our staff and, through the employees' attitude, the customer is positively disposed towards the company and its employees

It is much easier for a competitor to copy features of a product, imitate a service or utilise improved tools and equipment than it is to improve on the intangible elements; it is a much longer process which needs to be sustained continuously.

It is this feeling of customers that we really *care* about resolving the customer's issues which will create loyal customers who will come back and remain customers. In this context we should remember the long-established fact that it costs about five times as much to acquire a new customer than it does to keep an existing one.

Value added by customer care

Our customers are usually not looking for the 'cheapest' product with its connotation of low quality. What they are seeking is what they perceive to be the 'best value for money', which entails a much broader view of their needs. Some of these requirements may be real, others imagined, but to the individual customer the imagined need may be as important as the real one.

At the same time our product is, in most cases, not unique and the customer will therefore examine a number of suppliers' total offerings to find one which, in the customer's perception, satisfies most of his real or imagined needs. The customer will choose the supplier with whose total package he is most comfortable.

On the other hand, we must be able to satisfy these additional customer needs at a cost which the customer is willing to pay and which will be seen by the buyer as sufficient reason to use us or warrant our premium price. Satisfying these additional needs is seen by the customer as adding value to the basic product.

Satisfying some of these needs may be quite expensive for us.

Adding value through customer care, however, is unlikely
to add substantially to our costs and it may well be possible
to satisfy our customers' needs at the same or even lower
costs. In the following days we will discuss how this can be
achieved. In some instances there may be a need for some
initial expenditure or investment but it should be possible to
recover more than this outlay in the medium or longer term.
The aim of customer care is to make the customer feel good
about doing business with us.

All customers want to feel they are important and we must
therefore treat them as individuals to show them that they
are important. Without customers there would be no need
for our company's products or our own work.

Adding value through customer care is therefore a question
of doing our individual jobs as effectively as possible and
keeping the customer's needs in mind when performing
our tasks. Tomorrow, we will examine who our customer
really is.

The growing importance of customer care

Let us first of all list some of the main reasons for the
growing influence of customer care in the buyers'
purchasing decisions and then we will discuss each one of
them in more detail:

- Increased competition – the customer has a choice
- Better informed customers
- Product similarity – need to differentiate suppliers
- Rising demand for improved support

- Life cycle cost considerations – maintenance and running costs play an increasing part
- Integration of customers' own work with suppliers' products and services
- Desire to concentrate on own mainstream activities

Can you add to this list? Examine your own working environment and you will certainly come up with a number of additional reasons.

Let us expand on each of these points and let us start with, perhaps, the most important one.

Competition
It is only natural that where there is an attractive market, competitors will seek to obtain profitable business. The newcomer may sometimes even have an advantage due to the fact that he may have benefited from the experience of the established supplier. As the newcomers start from scratch, they can use the latest equipment, techniques and systems and can select staff to fit the image they wish to create.

Competition gives customers greater choice and they will therefore become more selective and knowledgeable about various suppliers.

The trend over the last few years has been to make many businesses work on a global basis, which further increases competition, not only from local sources, but also from overseas.

The creation of the European Union has made it easier to do business in all countries of the EU, and is thus not only offering an opportunity for companies to expand outside their own countries, but is also opening up the local market to competition from abroad.

We should not look at competition as something negative; it is likely to force our own business to become more efficient and is forcing many companies to become more customer orientated. This is a direction they should have taken in any case.

Better informed customers
Customers know a great deal more about our products and support activities than they used to, partly because of the above-mentioned competition and partly due to the extensive studies conducted by consumer groups, professional associations and other institutions. The media also tend to discuss in some depth the merits and demerits

of various products. A great deal of information is also available over the Internet (see Friday). The emphasis put into competitive advertisements also makes customers more aware of the aspects they should examine. The financial services industry is a good example, where public pressure has forced regulations on the industry, ensuring fuller disclosure of costs and more realistic estimates of benefits.

Product similarity
From the customer's point of view, it is difficult to distinguish many of our products from those of our competitors. They often use the same components and perform the same tasks in a very similar way. As an example, we could look at the personal computer industry, where a large number of computers can utilise the same software programs. One of the few ways we can differentiate ourselves from our competitors is by means of the image for customer care that we build up and the reputation for customer support that we have earned over time.

Rising demand for improved support
With the choice of supply sources now available to our customers they know that they are in a buyer's market and they are therefore demanding improved support from the suppliers they have selected. In general, it has been shown that with a higher living standard, customers are willing (and able) to pay for improved support. For instance, customers in the past may have been willing to wait for a week or two for a telephone to be installed whereas now they expect it to be done in as many days.

Life-cycle costs

As many products are technically more sophisticated, customers have become more dependent on the continuing support from us to keep their products in operation. They are increasingly looking at the life-time costs and our ability to support their products efficiently throughout the life of that product. When a customer buys a car, for instance, he will want to know how good the maintenance service is, what the costs are likely to be, the fuel consumption and the resale value after a certain number of years.

Integration of customers' own work with suppliers' products

As companies have come under greater pressure to cut costs, they have become aware of the need to integrate operations with those of their suppliers to simplify the work process. Let us examine two of these areas.

There has been a move towards suppliers delivering goods just in time (JIT) when they are needed by the customer. This has advantages for the customer, who does not need to hold large buffer stocks (less stock holding, no double handling, less obsolescence, less space requirement) but it puts pressure on the suppliers. They have to become more flexible in providing products when needed, the agreed quality has to be met all the time (rejects would immediately affect the customer's schedule) and delivery dates have to be strictly adhered to. For this service, customers are willing to pay a premium which is beneficial to both parties: the customer's savings far exceed the additional costs and the suppliers obtain a premium price for doing what they should have been doing in the first place.

The second major area is the integration of computer systems between customers and suppliers. In department stores, for example, the usage of stock items is automatically recorded. At suitable trigger points, orders are placed with the suppliers, goods are delivered, invoiced and paid for all without the involvement of repetitive human activities.

These trends have transformed the traditional adversarial customer–supplier relationship into a long-term *partnership* with greater interdependence.

Desire to concentrate on own main-stream activities
In the past, companies tried to do most activities in-house. They found that many tasks required professional skills which were not available inside the company and a great deal of management time was diverted into these activities. More recently these peripheral activities have been subcontracted to specialist companies who handle these tasks on behalf of the customer, either on the customer's own premises or elsewhere. This again requires a complete customer orientation in the supplier's company. Catering services are a typical example of this trend.

The role of the first-line manager

As we have seen earlier, customer care is partially a matter of skills, processes and tools, and partially a question of attitudes.

In both these areas, the first-line manager has a crucial role to play to ensure that senior management's intentions are suitably translated into actions where it really matters – where activities take place.

Our main tasks in orientating the company towards customer care

- Helping to identify the needs of our customers and understanding our company's desired position in the market
- Identifying employee skills strengths and deficiencies
- Ensuring that deficiencies are remedied (by training, counselling, reorganisation, reorientation, etc.) and that we build on strengths
- Establishing which processes and practices impede proper customer care and replace them by customer-oriented systems
- Examining current measuring systems to ensure they monitor customer satisfaction
- Recognising and rewarding good customer care performance
- Identifying issues in the process which impede good customer care and ensuring that these obstacles are removed
- Listening to customers, staff, colleagues and senior management and communicating on customer issues
- Leading staff by example
- Motivating staff to achieve customer satisfaction goals

This list could go on and on, but most of our tasks could probably be classified under one or the other of the above points. One of the difficulties companies have with implementing these tasks is that the authority vested in a first-line manager is often not sufficient to carry out all the above tasks efficiently.

We all know that senior managers have plenty of problems of their own and are not looking for additional ones. They will be much more willing to support any action proposed by us, if we can present to them not only the problem, but also a proposed resolution. Where other functions are involved, we should discuss the issues with them beforehand, and present an agreed proposal to senior management.

Company staff in direct contact with the customer (salesmen, service engineers, telephonists, delivery staff, secretaries, etc.) are often very well aware of the lack of customer support provided by the company. Their suggestions, however, are frequently not sought, and even where they are, they are sometimes ignored. If we give the matter a little thought, we will realise that these intelligent individuals, who are in daily contact with customers, are likely to be a very useful source of information about customer needs and of suggestions about how these requirements can be met. It is our role to release this valuable source for improving customer care by involving staff in discussions on this subject (we will learn more about this on Wednesday).

Our own organisation

The subjects we discussed today form the framework for the issues we will examine more closely during the rest of the week. Perhaps now is a good time for us to look at our own organisation, and specifically our own department, and ask ourselves a number of pertinent questions:

- Have we clearly defined what customer care means in our business?
- Are we aware that doing our work as efficiently as possible is not only adding to our company's profit but also to customer satisfaction, which will keep our company in business?
- Do we genuinely believe in the 'Customer is King' adage or are these only empty words?
- Are we concentrating only on our products or services, or do we analyse all our activities from the customer's point of view?
- When we look at the improvements introduced over the past two years, have they been generated primarily by internal needs or have they been customer orientated? Can we think of other improvements which will increase customer satisfaction?

- What are we doing to provide our staff with the relevant skills and aids needed for their job?
- Is the environment in our company conducive to a positive attitude of staff towards the company?
- Do we think we can compete effectively in a rapidly changing market without making radical changes in the way we view customers?
- How has our own role changed and how is it likely to change in the near future? How much effort is going into customer-orientated thinking?
- How well do we communicate? With customers? Within our own department? With other functions? With senior managers?

By thinking about these issues now will help us put what we will learn during the rest of the week into context.

Who are the customers?

Yesterday we examined customer care and its impact on
profits. We also established the reasons for its growing
importance and why action to improve customer care is
required *now*. We found that the first-line manager has a
crucial role to play in motivating his staff and helping with
the development of customer support programmes and in
their thorough implementation.
Today we will learn to:

- Identify our customers, both internal and external
- Establish customer needs
- Recognise everyone's role in customer care
- Use customer support as a competitive tool

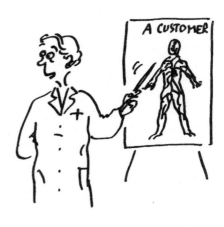

Who is my customer?

Don't let us dismiss this simple question without giving it a little thought. The immediate response is likely to be the end user of our product. On the path from the design of a product, through its various stages of manufacture, testing, packing, dispatching, storing, selling, invoicing, installing, servicing, collecting payment, etc. there is a long chain of activities. Each activity is performed by an individual or a group of individuals, and the output of this activity is used by someone else in the chain. Each recipient of this output *is a customer* and must be viewed just like an outside customer or end user.

Internal customers
It may not be easy to change our attitude to our colleagues by considering them to be our customers or our suppliers, whichever the case may be. But, if we want to support the end user adequately (and on Sunday we established the essential need to do just that) then we cannot ignore the intermediate links in the chain.

Staff in direct contact with customers cannot provide a good service to them unless they in turn are efficiently supported by their colleagues along the chain. We train our staff who are in direct contact with outside customers and end users in customer care skills. By using the same customer care skills on each and every internal customer, we will strengthen the whole chain, which will enable us to offer the end user a more complete support. The chain is only as strong as its weakest link.

You may accept that idea conceptually but you may have some difficulty in converting it into action-orientated programmes. One of the reasons for this hesitation may well be that it has not been done previously. Well, don't hesitate! It is much easier to identify internal customers and to establish their needs than it is for outside customers.

Who then is our internal customer? Just ask yourself the question. 'Who uses the output of my work?' and you have the answer. Everyone who uses the output of our work is our customer, be that person inside the company or an external user. Consequently, we often have a number of customers with possibly different needs and priorities.

External customers
It is not only the end user who is our customer. Obviously, it is the end user whose needs must be satisfied, as this is the ultimate source of our income. But there are often a number of intermediary customers who have their own needs which have to be satisfied. These intermediaries can be agents, distributors, franchisees, wholesalers, retailers or other types of middlemen. Needs of all these 'customers' must be satisfied.

Identifying customer needs

Now that we have clearly established who our customers really are, we must proceed to find out their genuine and perceived needs. Where internal customers are concerned we should first of all separate *needs* from their *wishes* and, by agreement with them, set about satisfying their genuine needs and setting aside the 'it would be nice to have' items. When it comes to external customers, whether they be the end users or intermediaries, it may be beneficial to satisfy both their real and perceived needs, as we may be able to gain a competitive advantage by catering for their perceived requirements as well, which may enable us to charge a premium price.

How do we set about identifying these needs? The obvious answer is to ask our customers and discuss their needs with them, so that we clearly understand what they really want. For this purpose it will be advantageous if we know as much about our customers' business as possible.

It is much easier to have this type of dialogue with an internal customer and yet we often fail to communicate adequately and in sufficient detail with our colleagues. The company frequently spends a great deal of effort and money in establishing external customer needs whilst ignoring the much simpler task of encouraging a similar approach to find out exactly what one person (or department) requires from another. Yet, unless the internal processes work satisfactorily, a favourable external result will be much more difficult to achieve.

This dialogue with our internal customers should result in a very clear specification of what the output of our work should be, its timing, frequency, amount of detail and to what standard the work should comply (see Friday). This specification should be reviewed at regular intervals, as changing conditions may affect out internal customers' requirements. For instance, it often happens that a statistical report or sales results are needed very frequently in the early stages of a product launch, but a longer interval between reports may be quite adequate at a later stage. If requirements are not regularly reviewed, company resources may be wasted.

Establishing external customers' needs is somewhat more complex as, in many cases, it will not be possible to ask each customer individually what his or her requirements are. A whole range of approaches is available:

- Direct discussion with customers
- Feedback from our own staff
- Analysis of customer complaints and comments (see Thursday)
- Market research
- Surveys
- Questionnaires (written, by telephone, personal interviews, internet)
- User-group discussions
- Customer audits
- Attitude surveys
- VIP visits to our premises

These alternatives can be used singly or in conjunction with one another and in some cases (e.g. attitude surveys) the trends are more important than the absolute figures.

Some companies are concerned that their customers will not be willing to discuss their needs with them. In practice, customers are only too willing to let us have this information if they believe that we will utilise it. It is up to us to build a sufficiently good relationship with our customers for them to realise that we are sincere in our desire to satisfy their needs and build a genuine partnership with them.

The quality of customer responses is likely to be varied. It is essential for these responses to be carefully analysed and, wherever appropriate, specific customer issues should be addressed immediately and progress communicated to the customer.

The same need for prompt response exists where we have received feedback from our own staff. Unless we keep the originator of the information fully informed of how the data has been used and what action we intend to take (or the reason for no action) the feedback will dry up. As the feedback is of such importance to us we must make sure of a continuous flow of information by showing our appreciation for this data to our staff.

The quest for updating our knowledge of customer needs, applications and satisfaction is never ending and continually changing. These changing requirements are influenced by the changing needs of our customers' markets and by the enhanced offerings provided by our competitors and ourselves. Yesterday's outstanding performance becomes today's standard and will be unacceptable tomorrow. If we want to succeed in our aim to delight customers, we will have to try to stay at least one step ahead of the competition.

Everyone has a role in customer care

Hopefully everyone in the company produces an output which is useful to someone else either inside or outside the company. If not, then maybe the job in question is superfluous. It is therefore necessary to recognise that by doing our work, we are contributing to the whole package of activities which make the customer want to continue doing business with us.

It follows that every member of the organisation has suppliers and customers and by agreeing in detail the output that will make our customers' work as efficient as possible will help us give satisfaction to our outside customers.

Using customer support as a competitive tool

It is not enough to provide excellent customer support – we also have to make it known to customers that we are doing so. Why is that necessary? Surely customers will know when they get superior service. It is a fact, however, that customer support is more apparent to customers by its absence than by its presence. Customers tend to take good customer support for granted, although experience should have taught them that this is not always the case.

Companies who provide good support have in the past few years learned to be forthcoming in letting existing customers, as well as potential new ones, know that the company takes customer support seriously. The way this has been done includes programmes such as:

- Customer charters
- Extended warranties
- Clearly stated performance standards
- Acceptance of penalties for non-compliance
- Return of money if the customer is not satisfied
- Publicity given to support provided
- Additional 'free' services (e.g. loan cars during maintenance of customer's vehicle)
- Customer helplines – carelines, Internet (see Friday)

It is becoming increasingly popular for key customers to be invited to act as a third-party reference in publicity material to highlight the benefit the customer has obtained by the support of the supplier. The partnership approach between customer and supplier is stressed. This is not only an excellent third-party reference for the supplier but, in addition, a good sales aid in the key customer's company, as the benefit of the support is brought home to a wide range of people in the customer's organisation, who may never have been involved with the support.

The difficulty quite often is with our own staff who take the excellent support we provide for granted, but do not adequately stress its benefit to the customer. It almost appears as if they are afraid of being boastful. Salesmen in one company, for instance, found it difficult to get a customer to agree to let his staff be trained free of charge in the supplier's local premises; they were concerned that the customer might object to releasing his staff for a day's training. Other salesmen in the same company used this training as a positive sales argument, stressing that the moment the customer's new equipment was installed on his premises, his staff would be ready to use it, and that the staff would make their mistakes on the supplier's equipment and not on the customer's newly installed one.

The message I want to leave you with is that customer support does not only need to be provided but that it also needs to be sold and marketed to achieve the full benefit of the activities.

Summary

Today we have:

- Identified our internal as well as our external customers
- Learned to establish customer needs
- Recognised the benefit of feedback from our own staff
- Come to realise that everyone in the company should be involved in customer care
- Examined ways of selling and marketing the benefits of superior customer support to existing and potential customers

Elements which influence customer care

Yesterday we learned to identify our customers along the whole chain of activities that help us to support the final users. We examined ways of identifying customer needs and how to use customer support as a positive selling and marketing tool.

Today we will go a step further and will study:

- The elements influencing customer care
- Customer care skills and attitudes
- Procedures and systems to assist us in customer care activities

Elements influencing customer care

As we saw during Sunday, the products provided by companies competing in any market are essentially similar and becoming more so every day. Customers' purchasing decisions are, therefore, influenced by elements other than the basic product. This is often referred to as the 'non-product value added' and comprises all the factors which go into demonstrating genuine care for the customer. It is a meaningful description of 'Customer Care', as it adds value to the customer beyond that of our product.

Let us first enumerate these elements and then examine each one in greater detail:

- The way the initial contact is handled
- The follow-up process
- Clear specification of product, features, price, payment terms, warranties, availability and after-sales support
- Simple ordering procedure
- Prompt order acknowledgement restating specification and terms
- Adherence to stated conditions
- Advance notice of any necessary deviation from conditions
- Assistance when product is delivered
- Clear invoicing – no hidden charges
- Easy access to supplier for assistance
- Opportunity to extend warranty, making service contract or other after-sales service activity
- Occasional after-sales contact
- All staff to be polite and helpful

These are just some of the most important elements
applicable to all businesses. Can you think of additional
ones applicable in your own environment?

Initial contact
A great deal of tact is required by our staff to ensure that the
customers realise they are being helped without getting the
feeling of being pressurised by the salesman. Our company
should have clearly laid down standards on how this very
important first contact should be handled (see Friday). The
first impression given to the customers at the time of the
initial contact is likely to remain with them for a very long
time and any bad impression will be difficult to eradicate.

Sometimes the first impression is created even before the
customer starts talking to a member of our staff. Aspects
which may influence this impression include cleanliness of
premises, environment of the reception area, customer
parking facilities, etc.

Not only do operational staff need to be trained in 'customer
handling skills' but management must also think 'customer'.

The follow-up process
Once the initial contact with customers has been made, we
must ensure that any queries which may subsequently arise
can be adequately dealt with by staying in touch with the
customer. The same comment concerning the need for tact
mentioned above applies. Customers must not get the
feeling that we are pressurising them as this would result in
the customer's genuine queries and concerns not surfacing
but being hidden by delaying tactics.

This is the time to convert the customer's fears of making the wrong decision into conviction that our product and its support is what is needed. Helpful advice can be decisive in a positive decision. Knowledge of the customer's products, industry and processes can be of immense help in enabling us to give customers confidence in the advice we are giving. This is why an increasing number of suppliers have industry-specific teams of experts to advise customers and potential customers. An honest approach is essential.

Clear specifications

Nothing is likely to annoy customers more than specifications of products and features which are vague or unclear, either deliberately or through carelessness. The same applies to pricing and payment terms, where some suppliers try to hide the fact that 'extras' are not standard equipment and have to be paid for separately. Even if customers do not complain, it leaves a bad taste in their mouths and they may not return to us for future purchases.

Warranties have also become a significant marketing tool in certain industries and clear identification of what is and what is not included in the warranty is essential. In this connection we should mention that the sale of extended warranties and other support activities, which become effective after expiry of the initial warranty, are becoming an increasingly profitable area of a manufacturer's or supplier's product palette, and here again, an absolutely clear statement of what is covered is essential.

A realistic date for the availability must be given to customers. Over-optimistic statements of delivery time will have a detrimental effect on the supplier's image in customers' eyes and may lead to major upsets. This is particularly important on products or services which tie into other activities or needs of customers.

Simple ordering procedure
This sounds an obvious point, but examine the difficulties some companies seem to put deliberately in the way of

customers wishing to place an order. In some instances, customers cannot use their own ordering procedures, but are asked to conform to those of their suppliers. They may have to complete complicated forms seeking unimportant information, which may have been useful in the past, but is of no conceivable use now.

Prompt order acknowledgement

The least we, as suppliers, can do to show gratitude to customers for having chosen us as suppliers, is to acknowledge the order promptly and to state clearly on it our understanding of what the customer ordered. This acknowledgement should leave no need for the customer to query it or for any vagueness which could lead to subsequent disputes.

Adherence to conditions

It goes almost without saying that it is essential to adhere to the terms and conditions agreed with the customer on the order and its acknowledgement. Customers have a genuine cause for complaint if we, the suppliers, do not respect the conditions and specifications of the order. Incidentally, it has been found by research that, where conditions are strictly adhered to the customers have no opportunity to query any points, they tend to pay more promptly, which has a beneficial impact on our cash flow. So don't give customers a chance to query or complain, and customers will be more likely to keep to the payment terms.

Advance notice of necessary deviation from conditions

On some rare occasions it may be impossible for us, as suppliers to meet all the conditions. One of the most usual deviations is a delivery promise which, for some reason or other, cannot be met. The essential part of customer care is not to wait till we have missed the promised delivery date (perhaps in the hope that the customer will not notice?) but to contact the customer immediately we find out that we cannot meet the promised date. This will enable a solution to be agreed between the customer and ourselves to minimise any problem that our missing the delivery date is likely to cause the customer.

Contacting customers before the event will also take the steam out of the situation as the customers will realise that we care about any problems we may cause, by trying to come to a mutually acceptable position to minimise them.

Assistance when a product is delivered
Some companies believe their task is completed when the product is delivered to the customer. This may be true in many industries, but in a number of others the customer needs advice or other help to become familiar with the product he has just bought. This assistance may take the form of training a customer's staff on how to operate the product, or it may require physical or verbal help in assembling the product to get it operational.

Operating manuals and installation instructions are often very difficult to follow, and in some cases, manufacturers have clearly not field-tested their manuals or instructions on lay customers. Customer care includes the supplier ensuring that the introduction of the product to a customer's premises proceeds as smoothly as possible.

Clear invoicing

Here again a clear statement of what the customer is asked
to pay for is essential. Great improvements have been made
over the past few years, but there are still invoices which
give only codes which are comprehensible to the supplier
but meaningless to customers. There are supermarket
printouts which do not itemise purchases or, worst of all,
invoices which try to confuse the customer in the hope that
he will not query extras, which he may have had a right to
assume would be part of the basic price. Often queries
directed to the Invoicing Department are answered by staff
who have not been trained in how to deal with customers
and who consider a call by a customer an interruption of
their 'real' work. Staff in these departments must clearly
understand that it is the customer who pays all our salaries,
and management must ensure that staff are properly
trained.

Easy access to the supplier
Customers must be able to contact the supplier not only
when they have an enquiry prior to purchasing a product,
but also after the sale. This is an area where immense
progress has been made by a number of progressive
companies through encouraging customers to contact them
by providing help centres, hot-lines and other tools which
enable customers to voice their opinions, get assistance and
feel that the company is genuinely interested in assisting
them. We will discuss these tools in greater detail on Friday.

Opportunity to contract additional services
Customers are increasingly calculating the life-cycle costs of
a product. They probably received meaningful data about
the acquisition cost, running costs and other expenses
involved in the early stages of a product, but they may find
it beneficial to be able to obtain from the supplier
information about extended warranties or service contracts
(which can be considered as an insurance cover against
expensive repair costs). They may also require information
about other after-sales maintenance alternatives (e.g. time
and material, exchange of modules, availability of upgrades)
or about advance training of their staff in operating the
equipment to its full potential, or in performing simple
maintenance tasks themselves.

Occasional after-sales contact
After customers have taken delivery of a product, suppliers
often forget about the original customer in their drive to find
additional customers. The customer feels abandoned by the
supplier. An occasional contact by the supplier will
strengthen ties between customers and suppliers, and when

it comes to upgrading the customer's product or to additional purchases, this cosseting of the customer will show a worthwhile pay off. This customer care activity will also favourably affect the attitude of the customer to the supplier, which will be useful when using the customer as a reference.

Dealing with customers
Although it should be obvious that all staff in contact with customers must at all times be polite and helpful, this is not always the case. Management must ensure that this prerequisite to good customer relations is clearly understood by everyone in the company. As we will see on Thursday, the attitude of staff will be strongly influenced by their attitude towards their employer. Their attitude, in turn, will be reflected in the way they communicate with customers.

Customer care skills and attitudes

To ensure a continuous high level of customer care, a persistent management and staff effort over time is required. It cannot be dictated from 'above' (although it must be driven by management) nor can it be introduced at short notice as a temporary measure. This is why organisations and brands try to differentiate themselves from their competitors by the quality of their customer care – it takes a long time and a great deal of effort to emulate the best practices of competitors. Customer care has to become an integral part of the organisation's thinking. Where specific problems are identified, companies often try crash actions to alleviate the situation, but these measures are usually only temporarily effective.

The approach should be a disciplined, well-thought-through, step-by-step progression:

- Developing and publishing a statement of the organisation's mission
- Incorporating customer care as an integral part of the strategy
- Preparing detailed plans of how to satisfy and exceed customers' identified needs
- Employing staff with positive attitudes and further improving their customer handling skills

Mission statement
The nature of mission statements (or statements of company philosophy) means that they must come from top management. The important issue here is that management must recognise that customer care is an essential part of reaching a company's profit targets and thus of the very existence of an organisation.

A study by two researchers, Frederick Harmon and Gary Jacobs, into the profitability of companies in their industrial groupings in the 'Fortune 500' list of companies showed that companies who had customer satisfaction as a priority issue in their mission statement were more profitable over a period of five years than companies who placed profitability at the top of their list. Many major organisations have used this study to review the visibility of customer satisfaction in their mission statement.

The crux, however, is not what management says, but how it acts to prove that the mission statement is not a mere platitude.

Incorporating customer care into the strategy
As we have just said, it is the *actions* of management which will influence the attitudes of people inside and outside the company. It is therefore necessary to integrate customer care thinking in all company strategies.

Incorporating customer-orientated considerations in all strategies does not mean that no decisions likely to be unpopular with customers will be made by management. For instance, it may from time to time be necessary to increase prices, which is bound to be unpopular with customers. What is important in these circumstances is for the customer to realise that he is still getting good value for money. Often our own staff are more resistant to a price increase than customers. The way we communicate the need for this increase to customers and to our own staff will affect its acceptability.

Developing detailed plans

To enable us to achieve the goals set out in the mission and in the strategy, we will have to develop detailed plans on how to satisfy and exceed customers' identified needs. Here the full involvement of staff from all areas of the company will be helpful. It is these employees, who are closer to the day-to-day tasks they perform, who will be able to contribute ideas for improvements in their field of expertise, which may help to affect customers' satisfaction with what we are providing to them.

These plans need to be developed across various functions so that improvements in one area do not unfavourably affect others, unless this is a calculated decision which will benefit the customer and/or our company. For instance, some companies have decided to reduce the number of their warehouses, which increases their transportation cost substantially. The resulting benefit was an improved level of logistic support to customers and lower total costs to the supplier. We will discuss developing customer care programmes and plans on Saturday.

Employing staff with positive attitudes and imparting customer handling skills

Greater emphasis is being placed in the recruiting process to ensure newly engaged staff have the right attitude towards the company and towards customers. In most instances, we also have existing staff, some of whom may have the right attitudes, whereas others may require guidance. Attitudes cannot be taught by management but management can positively (or otherwise) influence existing attitudes.

What can and must be taught are customer handling skills. Like most other activities, there are accepted ways of doing this, although these may differ in some detail from culture to culture, or even from industry to industry. In the past, companies have taught customer handling skills only to salesmen, who by the nature of their job are probably most familiar with how to deal with customers. More recently, customer handling skills are being taught to other staff in companies, including especially service engineers, receptionists, telephone operators, and accounting staff, as well as other administrative staff who may be involved in some contact with customers.

Procedures and systems

To complete the circle, company procedures and systems must also be made more customer and operator friendly. Staff will not be able to satisfy customer needs if the tools at their disposal do not allow them to do this efficiently (more about this on Friday). This means that internal procedures have to be viewed from the customer's point of view, and systems supporting these procedures must make them a real aid to assist our staff in helping customers and potential customers in their dealings with our company.

The personal touch in dealing with customers should be encouraged wherever possible, and certain information in the database should enable our staff to make customers feel like individuals, even though they may be dealing with a large organisation where they are used to being treated as a number. An insurance executive stated at a seminar that research carried out by her company had shown that customers who had dealings with the insurance company found that the *way* their issues were processed were almost as important as the outcome itself. Don't let out-dated procedures spoil our customer-orientated image.

Summary

Today, we identified 13 elements which influence the way customers regard our company and examined each one of these factors more closely.

We then realised that actions would not occur by themselves, and that we would have to work at changing attitudes and at imparting and reinforcing customer-handling skills in a wide range of our staff.

We found that top management has to initiate and support customer-orientated activities, and we identified four steps which had to be taken before we could effectively implement a customer-care programme.

Finally, we found that internal procedures and systems need to be reviewed from time to time to make them more customer and operator friendly.

Enhancing customer relations

We spent Tuesday learning about the elements which influence customer care. We found that these elements could only be implemented by staff exhibiting the right attitudes, having been taught the requisite skills to deal effectively with customers, and being supported by customer-friendly processes and systems.

Today we will progress to study ways of:

- Enhancing customer relations
- Improving communications
  - written
  - telecommunication
  - personal
- Developing a seamless organisation – team approach

Enhancing customer relations

It must be the aim of any company to create relationships with customers which will not only satisfy their immediate needs, but which will leave customers with a feeling of goodwill towards the supplier that will make them want to continue doing business with the supplier and sing his praises to the world in general.

This type of long-term relationship must be built on mutual trust and respect, which are created by adhering to the concepts learned yesterday.

Customers want to have relationships which will continue for a considerable time, where the supplier knows the customer's needs and the customer can rely on the supplier's assistance if and when required.

Let us assume the customer is a car manufacturer who purchases electric motors from a vendor. The electrical systems of a car on the drawing board today must be developed in parallel with the rest of the car. Who is likely to know more about electric motors, the car manufacturer or the manufacturer of the electric motors? It is therefore highly desirable to have the specialists from the manufacturer of electric motors working together with the designers of the car to come up with an optimal solution. This will, however, mean divulging sensitive information to each other and there must be complete confidence on both sides that the other will not use this information for improper purposes.

This frankness in a partnership relationship is not confined to technical information, it also often covers other areas of business, including finance. It has been known for financially strong customers to advance finance to vendors for, perhaps, capital investment in new machinery or a computing system, which uses the same architecture as that of the customer, to simplify administrative procedures on both sides.

To ensure all staff really enhance the relationship with customers, suppliers go to substantial lengths to check that the procedures and standards laid down are fully complied with. To demonstrate that their procedures are able to provide customers with the agreed standards, many companies seek accreditation to BS 5750 or its equivalent ISO 9000.

Company executives have at times been surprised when they telephoned their own offices that telephones were inappropriately answered, some calls were carelessly transferred to wrong departments or that the impatience of the telephonist or other recipient of the phone call is apparent from their voice. Some companies have made it a firm requirement for *all* executives, including the CEO (Chief Executive Officer) to spend a proportion of their time out in the field talking to customers and staff at the sharp end of the business. As one executive remarked, 'We cannot make meaningful strategic decisions about our business if we do not know what it is like to face customers.' In some companies senior executives from various disciplines are allocated a number of key customers with whom they keep in regular contact.

The 'mystery shopper' approach is used by a number of organisations to check compliance to customer care procedures. This can be done either by the company's own staff, but more frequently by employing an outside company to regularly check a range of preselected factors in the customer relation field.

As we have seen, enhancing customer relations consists of a number of tangible elements, but also of intangible elements which make customers feel comfortable in dealing with our company.

Communication

Let us first define what we mean by communication. Perhaps it is easier to start off by what communication is not; the passing of information in a single direction (e.g. an instruction down the line, or a report up the line) is highly important, but it is not communication. Communication is multidirectional or, at least, two-directional.

The danger of simply passing information from one person, one department, or one organisation to another is that the information may be misunderstood or misinterpreted, or be taken out of the context intended by the initiator.

Communication will hopefully eliminate, or at least minimise, any possible misunderstanding through the recipient's comments and the feedback received by the initiator. What is more, it is likely to lead to much more involvement in the common task by all persons concerned which, in turn, will lead to better decisions, greater commitment and thus more rapid and thorough implementation. In addition it is also motivational (see Thursday).

Let us examine ways we tend to communicate:

- By exchange of letters, faxes or e-mail
- By telecommunications
- By personal contact

Exchange of letters, faxes or e-mail
By the nature of this method of communication, the interchange of ideas and feelings is somewhat stilted and limited by the absence of an immediate response and of non-verbal indicators (e.g. smiles, hand movements, shrugs and other expressions conveying the other person's feelings). On the other hand, this written method gives the initiator the opportunity to review the message carefully before sending it, and there is a permanent record of it. Often letters and faxes are used to confirm an understanding reached by other methods of communication to combine the advantages of more than one way of communicating.

Telecommunication

This is a much more spontaneous way of communicating, as the interchange is instantaneous and the tone of voice helps in conveying some of the feelings which may not have been expressed in words. Because of this spontaneity, it is used increasingly in business, and the improvement in wired, as well as in cellular systems, is making the telephone an essential part of communicating with people inside and outside the company (see also Friday).

The disadvantage of the telephone for communication purposes is the absence of visual contact and the possibility of the recipient of our call to be caught unawares or be distracted by other activities in the office (or by traffic on the road if we reach the recipient while he or she is travelling). Also, there is no written record of the exchange of information, although in some organisations (e.g. banks, insurance companies, etc.) all telephone calls are automatically recorded. Linking computers with telephone technology now enables networking through the Internet (see Friday).

By personal contact
This is the oldest and most effective way of communicating with our staff and with customers and vendors. It is spontaneous, there is visual as well as audio contact, and there is a clear feedback of understanding or the lack of it.

Although there is generally no permanent record of the discussion (except where minutes are taken or a record is specifically requested by one or other of the parties), the outcome can be easily confirmed in a subsequent letter or fax. The main drawback of personal contact is the time and travel expense required for this method of communication.

Video-conferencing is trying to combine the advantages of personal contact with reducing the time and cost involved in travelling, but it is still a somewhat artificial way of making 'personal' contact.

Each of these methods of communication requires specific skills which we must teach our staff. Some of these skills (e.g. clarity and conciseness of expression) are common to all, others are specific to each method. It would lead into too much detail to cover these skills in this book, suffice it to say that material on all these skills is widely available. Here we are concerned with recognising the need to impart these communication skills to our staff.

One aspect that should be stressed is the real need to *listen* to the other party, be it a customer, a member of our own staff or anybody else. This means not only *hearing* (or reading) what the other party says, but trying to understand the intent of the communication and to take the idea on board. Too often the words are *heard* but the idea is dismissed without full consideration. What we *hear* is also coloured by our own experience and preconceived ideas so that we make no serious effort to consider the real intent of the message. I used to consider myself a good listener until I went on a 'Listening Course'. In the first hour of that course, it was proved to all participants that their perceptions coloured what they thought they had heard.

10 suggestions to improve listening
1 Listen for ideas, not just for words or reactions to persons
2 Take notes
3 Ask questions
4 Switch off your problems
5 Limit your own talking
6 Don't interrupt
7 Think like the customer
8 Don't jump to conclusions
9 Listen to overtones
10 Concentrate

It is estimated that 75% of a manager's time is spent communicating. This time is divided, as per recent studies, approximately as follows:

Listening	45–60%
Reading	4–19%
Talking	51–21%

This demonstrates the benefit of making some effort to improve our listening skills.

In this context we should also remember that communication conveyed by more than one sense is more likely to be remembered; it is therefore beneficial to combine the same message through a number of senses, e.g. through verbal communication and visual confirmation.

With the increasing use of the telephone mentioned earlier, many organisations are concentrating their training into this area. Precise guidelines are prepared on how the initial call should be answered, how it is to be transferred if this should become necessary, and the degree of formality that they wish to be used by their staff on the telephone.

For some unexplained reason, time wasted in waiting for the telephone to be answered or transferred is more aggravating than other types of delays and this needs, therefore, to be avoided by careful monitoring and planning. We will talk more on this subject on Friday.

The team approach

In today's complex business world it is often necessary to utilise experts in a number of different technical, financial, marketing, sales, administrative or other professional fields to enable us to serve the customer adequately. The customers, however, want to obtain an integrated recommendation from us covering all areas of expertise. Companies have realised this customer requirement for some time and have used specialists in various fields to assist the customer.

The difficulty that these companies experienced was the uncoordinated approach of all these experts, as each one advised the customer on the best approach relevant to his functional expertise, leaving the customer more confused than ever. Part of the problem was the functional organisational structure in most companies, and the allegiance members of particular functions had to their departments.

To overcome this difficulty, companies are increasingly structuring their organisations to reflect the customers' needs rather than their own internal requirements. This has meant creating teams of people from various specialised areas to work together on a customer project and present the customer with genuine solutions to problems. These teams are formed and disbanded as the needs dictated by customers' requirements arise. These more flexible structures give customers a really seamless image of a unified approach from the supplier.

Managing these teams from different professional disciplines requires a completely different management style. The professional guidance of team members is provided by someone outside the team whereas the (temporary) team manager may not have the professional functional skills of the individual team member. The team manager will, however, be very knowledgeable about the customer's industry and the specific needs of individual customers.

The skill of the manager is increasingly involved with encouraging (or motivating) the members of the team to work together for the benefit of the end result, which is to satisfy the customer and thus create additional profit for our company. The length of time team members will work together will differ depending on the type and extent of the project. The team may well consist of a number of permanent members and others that are co-opted for specific tasks for limited periods of time. Clearly, the difficult task of the team managers is to keep all resources and efforts devoted towards reaching the end goal. Tomorrow we will discuss some ways managers can motivate their staff or team members.

As in a football team, the strength of the team is dependent not only on the skills of the individual players but also on how well they work together. In the same way a project team must be fully integrated into the effort of supporting the customers' projects and must not press ahead with narrow, internal functional preferences to the detriment of the end result.

Summary

Today we concentrated our study on enhancing customer relations and the essential role played in this area by communication with customers, vendors, and our own staff.

We examined these methods of communication in some detail and identified advantages and disadvantages in each one of them. We came to the conclusion that, whenever really important information needs to be exchanged, a combination of methods is beneficial. We found that strained customer relations are often caused by an omission of concerted management action.

We then looked at the reasons why team work has become essential in today's environment and we examined the current moves towards a more flexible, seamless organisation. Not surprisingly, we found that the task of managers in this flexible team structure has changed and necessitates a greater orientation towards customers.

Complaints

Yesterday, we examined ways of enhancing customer relations. We found that communication was an essential skill all of us have to use to keep customers happy and to form long-term partnerships with them. We came to the conclusion that in modern businesses, a team approach was necessary to ensure best advice to customers, and we had to find ways of presenting a united front to the customer.

Today we will examine:

- Complaints
  - complaints handling
  - complaints management
  - the role of management
- Motivation
- Brainstorming

Complaints

In the past, management often tried to avoid complaints being made by customers and when they were being made, they were dealt with at a management level as far away as possible from senior management.

During the last decade or two, more and more companies have come to realise that complaints are a valuable way of establishing customer needs and hearing their opinions and comments about our products and services. Companies now tend to spend a great deal of money and effort to encourage customers to complain and comment.

Why has there been such a drastic change of approach to complaints? As we have seen earlier, it costs on average five times as much to acquire a new customer than it does to retain an existing one. Furthermore, existing customers tend to spend more with us than new customers and they are likely to remain more loyal to our company or to our brand.

Other studies have shown that only a relatively small percentage of dissatisfied customers will actually make a complaint which would give us the opportunity to put matters right and turn them into satisfied ones. The great majority of customers will simply vote with their feet and not come back to us; they will, however, tell their friends and colleagues about their real or imagined grievance without giving us a chance to comment.

Encouraging customers to complain
Having come to the conclusion that we *want to encourage* customers to complain we have to find ways of doing so. Some companies go to extreme lengths and substantial costs

to make it easy for customers to complain or make their views known. Let us mention just a few here:

- Stamped and addressed cards supplied with products or easily available at point of sale
- Free-phone help-lines manned for long periods of the day
- Customer service desks at point of sale
- Approach after the sale by the supplier or manufacturer to the customer to check satisfaction
- Offer of exchange or money back if not satisfied

Having initiated actions to encourage customers to complain, we must have a quick and easy follow-up procedure for dealing with these complaints. We can divide the actions we must take into two distinct areas: the handling of complaints and the management of complaints.

Handling complaints
This is the immediate action required to pacify the customer and to resolve or, at least mitigate, the issue. Customers are often almost as concerned about *how* their complaint is dealt with as they are with the final outcome itself. There are six basic rules:

- Listen
- Probe
- Agree solution
- Adhere to agreed solution
- Follow up
- Implement escalation procedure if necessary

Listen   Nothing is likely to make customers more angry than if the person they complain to does not pay full attention to what is being said or, worse still, interrupts on the assumption that the issue has already been understood. The message is, listen, do not interrupt, take notes and show sympathetic interest. We must always remain calm and polite.

Probe   The facts have to be established in some detail and it will usually be necessary to ask questions to avoid misunderstandings and to get the complete picture. In some instances, this questioning may resolve the issue by highlighting some action the customer may have omitted to take or an explanation which has been misinterpreted. The probing should proceed in a systematic way to enable the next step to be undertaken.

Agree solution   Having elicited all relevant facts, we are now in a position to propose a solution which is agreeable to the customer. We may not be able to resolve the issue completely on the spot but we can probably find an interim solution which is acceptable to the customer until the matter is finally resolved. This agreed solution should be very specific, and it must not leave the customer in any doubt as to what to expect.

Adhere to agreed solution   We certainly do not want to exacerbate customers further by letting them down a second time. It is essential to ensure that every detail of the promised solution is fulfilled. It is not good enough simply to request another department to perform some action – we have taken on the responsibility on behalf of the company to take certain actions, and we must ensure that they happen. We have to get the firm commitment of any other person or department involved that the remedial action will be taken, and we must check that this is performed to the agreed standards and schedule.

Follow up   Once we have ensured that the agreed solution has been fully implemented, it is recommended practice for us to contact the customer again to get a positive agreement that we now have a satisfied customer again. A clear procedure must be laid down in our company to make sure that this additional step is taken to demonstrate our involvement with the customer's problem. Customers who have had a complaint and who have been fairly and quickly dealt with will become loyal clients in the future, and they will be happy to recommend our company to other potential customers.

Escalation procedure   It is not always possible to come to an agreed solution with a customer. Most customers are reasonable people to deal with, but there is always the odd exception to every rule. For this reason, and because some issues may have to be resolved at a higher management level, escalation procedures should exist and should be implemented in all appropriate circumstances. On the other hand, we should empower our staff who are dealing with complaints, to enable them to come to an agreed resolution with the customer on the spot. In a survey by British Airways, it was found that travellers who had a complaint, wanted it resolved by the person they were talking to without having to have the matter referred to higher authority. The high priority given to this customer requirement in the survey was a surprise to the company, and a change was initiated as part of their customer care programme.

Managing complaints

Once the immediate 'fire' has been put out we must take further advantage of the complaint by examining the underlying cause of it to ensure it does not occur again. In the past, companies resisted this type of investigation as they felt that a 'witch hunt' after the event was not going to bring them much benefit. With the recent drive for excellence, they have found it essential to establish the root cause of the complaint and to take appropriate action (even if that action is a considered decision not to take any action).

This is not as simple as it sounds, in view of the fact that a number of different departments may be involved and their short-term priorities may be different to those of the person trying to resolve a complaint. That is the reason why management must develop, publish and thoroughly implement procedures to ensure that issues are followed through to their logical conclusion.

The approach often taken is based on the team approach we examined yesterday. Representatives of various departments involved form a team to study the basic cause of individual complaints and agree solutions and their timing. This has led to substantial improvements in the operation of companies, which has more than paid for the costs involved in handling and managing complaints. It has also had the additional, non-quantified benefit of enhancing customer satisfaction which brings with it consequent marketing advantages to the company.

The role of management
In well-run organisations, customer complaints are being taken very seriously. It is usual to have a senior executive take charge of coordinating all activities involved in handling and managing complaints (not necessarily on a full-time basis) and for him to have to report to the board of directors on various aspects pertinent to complaints on a regular basis.

Motivation

This is a subject which behavioural scientists study all their lives and we will not attempt here to turn ourselves into specialists on motivation. On the other hand, we need to know how to apply motivational theories to the practical task of motivating customer care staff. Let us accept that in our company the 'hygiene factors' (those factors which cause dissatisfaction among employees if they are absent or inadequate but which will not positively motivate them if they are further improved) are satisfactory. We can only start motivating our staff once this stage has been reached.

Behavioural scientists agree that all of us are motivated by certain factors, but each one of us may have a different mix of priorities and motivators. Below is a list of some of the most important motivating factors:

- Involvement
- Achievement
- Recognition
- Feeling of belonging

Let us examine each of these in a little more detail to see how we can motivate our customer care staff.

Involvement
All of us want our ideas to be thought worthwhile and to be considered seriously. Managers often underestimate the wealth of knowledge and genuine interest of their employees. It is up to us, the managers, to harness this

knowledge and to get our staff to put forward their ideas. We have to encourage our staff to do so actively. From past experience, employees know that managers have tended to trivialise suggestions by their staff or, worse still, to ridicule the person who had made the suggestion. This has led to a reticence from staff to put ideas forward publicly; instead, staff tend to grumble among themselves, adversely affecting morale.

To overcome this natural reticence and to release the potential inherent in our staff, we have to encourage them to get involved in generating ideas, to be willing to express their opinions freely and without fear of negative reactions from their managers or colleagues. Various formal and informal methods are used to encourage this involvement but the most important one is the attitude of the individual manager and the whole management team.

Once this attitude exists, the following methods are used singly or jointly by various companies to get their staff to contribute their ideas:

- Small work-group meetings
- Formal suggestion schemes
- Quality circles
- Brainstorming sessions
- Managers' open-door policy
- Cross-functional assignments
- Managers talking and listening to their staff
- Open communication flow

Achievement

We spend a great part of our waking life at work and we all want to take pride in what we are doing. To enable us to be proud of our work, we not only need the recognition of our managers and colleagues, but we also need to get a feeling of satisfaction at having achieved something worthwhile.

To enable us to recognise that we have achieved something, our goal must be clearly established. This goal should not only be a long-term target with, perhaps, a one-year time horizon but should consist of short-term, intermediate goals or milestones against which we can measure ourselves along the way.

One of the most widely used ways for employees to be able to get a feeling of achievement is a regular performance review by their manager. During this review the employee and the manager agree performance targets and standards for the next period, and achievements since the last review are discussed. Targets should be challenging, but they must be achievable.

It also makes all of us feel satisfaction if we, or our company, contributes something to society, the environment, the Third World, etc.

With the current drive for 'flatter' organisational structures, there is a need for more genuine delegation by the manager, which is likely to have beneficial effects on the motivation of the employee. Delegation is a skill in its own right which we, as managers, must acquire. Delegation does not mean telling the employee step by step how the job should be done; that is instruction. On the other hand, neither is it to throw a task at the employee and then ignore him until the task is completed; that is not delegation, that is abrogation.

Recognition
Having achieved our goal, it is always pleasant to have one's achievements appreciated by others. Here again we, the managers, have a role to play. The most basic requirement is for recognition to be genuine, i.e. only real progress should be praised. The second desirable step is for recognition to be as public as possible. Let us keep to the dictum, 'Praise in public and criticise in private'. So many of us tend to do exactly the opposite.

Feeling of belonging
This is a difficult one! This type of feeling cannot be
generated at short notice. It is based on an attitude of trust
by management in their staff which is usually reciprocated
by the employee's loyalty to the company. It takes time to
engender this type of an attitude but it can be destroyed
quite quickly. Most of us like to be team players; we want to
belong to a group of which we can feel proud. It is our
management task to build this team spirit to ensure
everyone in the company is pulling in the same direction.
Some of the methods used to generate a feeling of belonging
include:

- Free communication and involvement
- Shedding the 'them and us' distinction between
  management and staff
- Public recognition of achievement
- Company social and sports activities

It is essential for each of our staff to understand that
managers' achievements are measurable as the sum of the
achievements of all their staff, and thus everyone
contributes with his performance to the end objective. Once
this is understood, the constructive criticism by the manager
will be more readily accepted as a move towards
improvements desired by everyone concerned.

Brainstorming

We mentioned brainstorming as one of the techniques that
can be employed to encourage involvement of our

employees in the company's activities. Let us examine some basic rules of brainstorming:

- Select people who can and are willing to contribute
- Allow adequate time
- Choose an appropriate subject and put it on a clipchart
- Explain that everyone should contribute ideas but that no discussion will take place at this stage
- Brainstorm for 30 minutes and list every idea put forward on the clipchart
- Get participants to indicate which of these ideas they feel should be pursued as a priority
- Divide participants into three groups and ask each group to develop a detailed plan for implementing one of the three ideas given the highest score by the participants

Summary

We covered a lot of ground today. We looked at distinguishing between handling complaints and managing them, and we examined how we could use complaints in a positive way to form a closer bond between our customers and ourselves. We found that we could get the greatest benefit from complaints only if senior management showed their interest in resolving issues that have been highlighted by the complaints.

This led us onto the subject of motivation of our staff. We identified some of the major motivating factors, and we went on to examine practical ways of implementing activities which would support these factors.

Finally, we went into some detail of how to employ the brains and knowledge of our employees by discussing brainstorming and the need for proceeding in an organised fashion. This will give us the greatest benefit from the resources we are going to invest in this activity.

Setting and measuring standards

Yesterday we studied ways we could use complaints to help us prove to customers that we genuinely want to satisfy their needs and how these same complaints could be used to stimulate our continuous improvement process throughout the company. We found that to do so, we needed to motivate our staff and so we examined how we could apply standard theory on motivation to our customer service staff. We concentrated on involving them in the decision-making process and described an approach to brainstorming. Today we will cover:

- Management tools
- Setting standards
- Measurement of results
- Feedback and use of data

Management tools

Whereas the principles of customer care do not change too much over the years, customer expectations and the tools available to management to satisfy customer needs and expectations are changing very rapidly. We have covered how we identify these needs and expectations and now we will concentrate on the multiplicity of new technological aids that have become available during the past few years. As with all technologies, they tend to be expensive at the beginning and are therefore used by the larger enterprises only but as they become more widely used they become more cost effective even for smaller companies. These tools are making the provision of customer care and its benefit to our company a practical proposition but we must not get blinded by technology itself; we must always look at these tools as mere aids to achieve our customer care goals. We should mention here, right at the beginning, that these management tools should be integrated, wherever possible, with other company processes to gain the maximum benefit for the whole enterprise. We must remain sensitive to customers' real requirements and accept that some of them will require help from us before they can be comfortable using these new technologies and management concepts.

Customer Care Centres
There has been a phenomenal growth of these centres over the past few years. They started off as simple Help Desks, Dispatch Centres, Logistic Units, Response Centres and have now developed into full blown Customer Support Centres, Knowledge Centres, and Single Point of Contact.

Despite a great deal of automation, this remains a very labour intensive activity. At the end of 2001 there were approximately 400,000 people employed in Customer Care Centres in the United Kingdom. To put this number in perspective, it means that there are more people employed in Customer Care Centres in Britain than in the coal, steel and car manufacturing industries combined. However, it is anticipated that this number will reduce over the next few years as many of the Customer Centre activities will be carried out on a global basis from centres in low-cost countries such as India, where low labour costs are combined with a good telecommunication infrastructure and a well educated labour force.

These centres utilise a combination of many technologies: telephone, e-mail, fax, internet (web forms, web chat, 'Call me' button, voice over internet), interactive TV, WAP (wireless application protocol), PDA (personal digital assistant). The choice of channels available to individual customers is an important consideration. It is not unusual to make a value segmentation of customers, where, for instance, the highest value customers get the best level of service (e.g. field visits, co-browsing, phone calls) whereas lower value customers are made more profitable by more cost effective channels (e.g. web self-service or interactive TV.)

A recent survey carried out on Customer Care Centres has shown that they perform a useful, primary function, but that the wealth of knowledge and data available in these centres is not fully integrated with other company activities and processes and that the enterprise is thus obtaining only part of the benefit of the system.

On the one hand, if we wait till the complete integration has been carried out, we will not implement the system on time. It is preferable to plan for total integration but implement some of the parts more rapidly to gain an early benefit for the customer and for our enterprise. On the other hand, a bad experience will turn a customer away.

M-business

Mobile business – giving direct access to information while on the move – has become an accepted way of life for busy executives. Advanced mobile phones can access information through GSM (global systems for mobiles), GPRS (general packet radio service), WAP (wireless application protocol), SMS (short message service) and mobile ticketing has made great strides. However, many businesses are not convinced about upgrading to 3G, as the cost/benefit ratio of third generation has not yet been generally proven.

The Web

In recent surveys it has been shown that the main reason why enterprises have invested heavily in websites is to improve their service to customers, followed a close second by cost savings and new revenue opportunities. These websites have to be carefully designed to enable customers to obtain the information they are seeking quickly and easily, without having to search around for a long time, i.e. it must be designed around customer needs. The website needs to be integrated with core company applications to be able to support customers adequately. That is the reason why many companies have developed personalised web pages that fit customers' unique needs and thus making it easier for customers to obtain the information they need. It is also an excellent data base for the supplier and it creates loyalty from customers. By watching where customers go on the website (their 'click behaviour') an enterprise can perform 'click stream analysis' to determine customer preferences. It is essential to analyse the information gained from the web to take full advantage of the system.

Integration

As we have seen in the previous paragraphs, a number of different media are used in supporting customer activities. To get the full advantage of this multimedia approach the systems must be integrated, analysed and utilised. Some of the management tools which used to be stand-alone systems, now form part of a seamless approach to customer issues. The control of response times is an important tool for companies who have to control staff movements in the field, e.g. companies servicing equipment in the field, the tracking of police, ambulance or fire fighting staff and vehicles, monitoring taxis, etc. These programs log each request for attendance, prioritise calls within geographical areas, estimate the time of arrival, notify the appropriate unit to perform the requested activity, note the time of arrival, the activity performed, the parts used and the availability for further activities. This system is probably linked to the administrative system, which will automatically invoice the customer (if appropriate), record and replenish spare parts used, and, if necessary, order replenishments. Other administrative systems link the customers' and the suppliers' systems, so that orders are placed automatically at predetermined stock levels, delivered and invoiced without any paper work being generated.

As customers are particularly sensitive to having to wait for telephones to be answered and the way calls are handled, equipment has been developed which measures the time customers had to wait for their call to be picked up, the length of the call and the time and day of the call so that management action can be taken to smooth out peaks and troughs in activities. Nothing is likely to be more off-putting to a customer than to receive the message 'Your call is important to us, please stay on the line and your call will be answered as soon as an operator becomes available', over and over again. This may turn him/her into an ex-customer.

Care must be taken not to depersonalise the transactions excessively, as contact with the customer remains essential for good customer relations. The skill of management is to find ways of employing management tools effectively to improve customer care and profitability and, at the same time, keep in close contact with the customer. By using these tools effectively it will tie customers more closely to their suppliers.

Setting standards

It is important to agree standards for as many activities as possible. These standards need not be set to provide the highest quality at any price – they should be set to meet or exceed customer-agreed requirements. If no additional benefit is gained by us or the customer by setting an even higher standard, which may be expensive to achieve, then it would be wasteful to do so. On the other hand, if setting and conforming to a higher standard will give us a competitive advantage, we must carefully calculate the additional costs and balance these against the potential benefit.

If no standards are set, then each event will be determined by the prevailing attitude of the employee in question or the time which happens to be available. We cannot leave as important a factor as customer satisfaction to chance, and we must therefore set performance standards on individual tasks. It is similar to the process control approach in manufacturing, where we try to deviate from within our standard limits as little as possible in order to give customers a uniform quality. In our case, the standards should be customer oriented and should be based on customer-expressed requirements. With the modern management tools available to us it is possible to measure achievements of many of these standards quite easily and, at the same time, to cater for customers' varied needs by agreeing relevant standards for individual requirements. We can use best practices of other companies to benchmark our own performance.

In an endeavour to provide customers with the level of support they require, many companies now give the customers options as to which level is most appropriate to their specific operation. For instance, health insurance companies offer their customers full private hospital cover or, for a reduced cost, similar cover if a National Health Service hospital cannot treat the patient within six weeks. Another similar example would be the laundry in a hotel, where the standard service may be for return within 24 hours but for an additional charge an express service is available for return within eight hours.

In support activities, customers can often choose a level of service or response and pay according to the level chosen. All these activities need standards to be set and conformance to these standards to be monitored. An ever-increasing number of organisations have developed 'Customer Charters' which set out standards for major factors important to the customer, and often these organisations accept penalty clauses which offer customers some compensation if the organisation fails to perform to the set standards. Examples of standards:

- Time required to answer a telephone call
- Time to respond to a letter or fax
- Time required to resolve a problem
- Frequency of management visits to customers
- Anticipated time between breakdowns (MTBF = mean time between failures)
- Mean time to repair (MTTR)
- Frequency at which sites should be inspected for safety, cleanliness or other relevant factors
- Length of queues
- Response time to request for service

When we set these standards it is important that we should understand what effect conforming to these standards will have on the customers and on ourselves, and we must ensure our ability of maintaining them. Let us take the first standard in our list and examine it a little more closely.

It is not enough to set only an average time for answering a telephone call; we must also specify the distribution of time around the average.

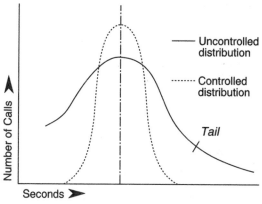

Distribution around an average

Let us assume that the average time to respond to a call is 10 seconds from the moment of the first ring. In an uncontrolled system this distribution is likely to have a number of calls replied to within three or four seconds and a 'tail' of a small number of calls which may take several minutes to be answered. Individual customers are not really interested in our average. What they want to know is how long they have to wait. It is no use to point out to them that other customers (or even they themselves at another occasion) had their call answered promptly.

In consequence, our standard, in addition to giving the average, should also give a maximum time to ensure that a more normal distribution is achieved. By cutting off the 'tail' we are going to get more satisfied customers because they are getting a more even service. In both cases the average is 10 seconds but the standard deviation is different. You may know the story of the person having one foot in freezing

water and the other in hot water – the average temperature may be a pleasant 30 degrees Centigrade but the person will be very uncomfortable.

The same approach applies to most of the standards mentioned. In some exceptional circumstances it may not be possible to meet the agreed standards. In these, hopefully rare, instances it is essential whenever possible, to inform the customer prior to the occurrence or deadline that there will be a variance from the agreed standard and a mutually acceptable solution will, in most cases be found (see Wednesday). Customers will be much less tolerant if the standard agreed is not met without prior indication of this happening.

To summarise our finding on standards, standards should be:

- Challenging but realistic
- Meaningful to customers and to our customer care vision
- Measurable wherever possible
- Regular audit and feedback is necessary

Measurement of results

Once we have agreed standards, it is necessary to know how we are going to measure them, the frequency with which we will do so and what we will do with the results.

Measuring against standards has been aided immensely by the use of modern management tools. In the past it would have been economically impossible to measure many of the activities now considered essential for satisfying customers. To use the same example as earlier in this chapter, measuring the time customers have to wait before a telephone call is answered and plotting distribution of telephone calls would have been difficult two or three decades ago, but now it can be done at a very reasonable cost. But just measuring what is happening is of a little use to us unless we propose to do something positive to affect the situation.

To come back to our example. Let us assume that our early measurements show us that we have an uncontrolled condition with an unacceptably long tail as shown in our diagram. One way to resolve the situation would be to get more telephone operators and install more telephones lines, but this is likely to be an expensive solution. By studying the pattern of incoming calls, the source of calls, the distribution during the hours of the day and similar factors, more cost-effective solutions are feasible. It is usual in most businesses that the pattern of calls differs substantially between certain hours of the day, days of the week or season of the year, enabling us to establish a clear trend. The source of calls may also show a 'bunching' of customer and employee calls at the same period.

The job of a manager is, not surprisingly, to manage. To do that, managers need information. Once the information is to hand, it needs to be analysed before ways of improving the situation are planned and action-oriented decisions taken. To continue with our example, the manager may decide to organise the company's own staff to telephone at low activity periods (troughs on distribution graphs), flexible work hours may be introduced to give better coverage during peak periods, holidays or days off can be planned to avoid periods of peak activity, staff from other areas can be drafted at peak periods into relevant areas, or calls lasting a longer time can be transferred to other departments.

The essential points we need to bear in mind on measuring activities are:

- What gets measured gets done
- Results may be gradual – follow trends as well as absolute figures
- Establish causes of variance (variance analysis)
- Data is only useful if it is utilised

Feedback

To obtain the basic data, we need feedback from customers as well as from our own staff. Unless we demonstrate via senior management actions that we take the comments made by customers and staff seriously, the flow of information will dry up. Conversely, if we can show that we use the information to improve our customer care, the flow will continue.

Let us now look at ways some companies use to encourage feedback:

- Personalised letters
- Management visits to customers
- Short lines of communication, quick decisions, delegation
- Managing complaints
- Customer help-lines (careful monitoring of comments)
- Customer surveys, questionnaires, audits
- Staff training and development
- Ideas workshop (caring approach but avoid 'wish lists')
- Employee surveys
- Involvement
- Good database which is actively used

Summary

Today we discussed management tools used in improving customer care. We found that these systems can be used directly to improve customer support and thus indirectly help our sales effort. Using these tools effectively has also enabled us to use them as a direct means of improving the whole management process and tie the customer more closely to our company. Pressure on profit margins has encouraged more and more companies to use these tools to enable them to provide the necessary level of customer support without increasing costs.

To achieve this we also examined how to set standards which must be customer oriented to provide the maximum benefit. From these customer centered standards, susidiary internal standards are set which should be specific and measurable wherever possible. We then went on to examine various methods of how to use these measures to improve our operation. We found that feedback from customers and from our own staff was essential and we looked at various ways of encouraging feedback.

The customer care programme

During the last six days we have been examining individual aspects affecting customer care. Yesterday we discussed the more widely used management tools to facilitate customer care and how to use these tools for improving efficiency and as aids for selling and marketing. We concentrated on setting standards, measuring against these standards and on how to utilise information and data obtained.

Today we will put the individual items together into a total customer care programme.

We will look at ways of:

- Developing a coherent customer care programme
- 'Selling' this programme inside the company
- Developing action plans
- Implementation
- Building on success

Developing a customer care programme

Here is an example of the development of a customer care programme:

- Analyse current customer care requirements of the market
- Establish our own position
- Specify desired position
- Identify our options and the relevant resource requirements to move from our present to the desired position
- Select options we will pursue
- Scrutinise 'best practice' in customer care areas selected (benchmarking)
- Appoint working parties to progress specific options selected
- Review results of working parties and develop a company-wide customer care plan
- Assign individual responsibilities for developing action plans and standards for each task
- Develop an implementation plan
- Implement (fully or on a test basis) the plan
- Monitor initial results and adapt programme as necessary
- Review at frequent intervals and provide feedback throughout the organisation

We will not examine each of these steps in detail, as most of them have already been discussed during our earlier studies this week. However, there are just a few additional comments which may help us in developing a coherent customer care programme.

- We must be brutally honest when examining our own business and realistic about its achievable progress
- We must utilise all the company's knowledge and skills by involving as wide a range of staff in developing and implementing our plans as possible
- We must prioritise our options not only by their financial benefits, but we should start by selecting projects for initial implementation which will give us positive results in a relatively short time, to encourage further activities
- We must have a clear idea of what the desired aim of a project is and brief our staff accordingly
- We must make sure that adequate manpower and financial resources are made available for progressing the customer care programme, as well as for continuing our day-to-day activities efficiently in all units
- We must keep our staff fully informed of progress at every stage of the programme and ensure their continued commitment to improve customer support. Concentrate on how these improvements have been received by customers. To use Tom Peters' dictum: '*Celebrate success*'

Internal selling

In most organisations there will be people who will overtly or covertly take a negative stance to any new programme which leads to change. We must not allow these attitudes to dampen the enthusiasm of other members of staff, but must take suitable steps to discuss these matters with them privately and specifically ask for their personal involvement, pointing out our need to utilise their skills and knowledge to further the aims of the company. We should make them responsible for progressing certain activities which they can call their own, and we should make them feel an essential part of the team. We should welcome any constructive criticism from them, but we must not allow negative attitudes to infest the rest of our staff. Managers must learn to deal sympathetically but firmly with these individuals.

It is not only members of the staff that need to be persuaded that their personal involvement in developing and implementing customer care programmes is necessary. Senior management knows that there is a direct link between service and revenue. Good customer service is not offered out of altruism. Some members of senior management may need to be persuaded that their personal commitment is essential and that platitudes will no longer be sufficient. It is often more difficult to show management in successful companies that change is necessary, as they feel that what has worked in yesteryear will also work in the future. Managers in unsuccessful companies know that radical change is required. More recently all managers have come to realise that they must move with rapidly changing customer requirements and expectations.

How do we demonstrate to senior management that their full commitment to customer support activities is essential? Top management have a large number of activities to coordinate and have to take decisions on many matters. They don't need any more problems! If we raise new issues with them, they want us also to present them with solutions.

Therefore, give them solutions:

- Quantify profit impact of customer satisfaction
- Identify whole spectrum of support needed to satisfy customers
- Present proposed approach to reaching solution
- Indicate likely financial and manpower resources required and time horizon

> • Convince senior management to think of themselves
> not as providers of products but as providers of
> service

The most difficult part of selling the need of this programme
to top management is to get a hearing. Here we need to use
shock tactics by showing the reduction in profit currently
caused by dissatisfied customers.

The next step is to demonstrate that we have given this
matter considerable thought by presenting to them the
approach outlined in the previous section.

Finally, obtain top management's full commitment to
support the programme and have a member of the top
management team identified who will take personal
responsibility for steering the programme through every
nook and cranny of the company.

We need to talk the language of senior management, a
language they understand: *profit*. We should be able to

demonstrate that lack of customer satisfaction is incurring additional costs to us (dealing with complaints, putting things right after they went wrong, finding new customers to replace those that moved away, etc.) and that it also loses us revenue through dissatisfied customers voting with their feet.

Top management will readily understand that satisfied customers are likely to provide us with more profit than dissatisfied ones. Often they do not appreciate that to satisfy customers more is required than a good product, a low price and a forceful sales force. This is the area where we must show that the loyalty of customers demands more than that; customers must be able to rely on the total support of their suppliers to work efficiently. We will have to convince all doubters that this requires a team effort.

Implementation

Many good programmes have failed due to sloppy implementation of the plans. Management often consider their work complete when the programme has been developed and approved. The benefit of the programme will only show after implementation and a great deal of attention needs to be exerted to ensure that it is implemented as planned. Any deviation should be fully documented and agreed to ensure that we know exactly what we are evaluating. Management responsibility should be clearly defined. Management needs to motivate staff continually to maintain commitment to the programme. Interest levels often fall once the excitement of developing the plan has been completed. Have fun!

Building on success

Customer care does not have an immovable goal. The moment we reach our current targets, the goal posts change, and further improvements have to be made to keep up with a changing market-place and more demanding customer expectations

We have to build on our success, remotivate our team, recognise and reward achievements and encourage creativity.

Open communication with our customers and our staff should help us identify our joint achievements, and it is up to us to use all the methods discussed throughout this book to rekindle the fire of enthusiasm to discover additional ways of cementing our partnership relations with our customers. Like a rose garden, this relationship needs continual tending.

We should not rely on this happening on its own; we will have to actively promote continued improvements in this area. Customer care is an ongoing activity which cannot be done once and just ticked off as completed.

Summary

We have spent the week examining various aspects of customer care. We started the week by trying to understand customer care in general and its impact on company profits in particular. We also enumerated some of the main reasons for its growing importance in strategic and operational considerations. We then considered the first-line manager's role in reorientating the company towards customer care.

On Monday, we identified the need, not only for direct customer support, but also for support from staff further removed from customers; we introduced the concept of the internal customer. We went on to recognise the need for information on customer requirements and how to establish what these requirements were.

We then went on to study the elements influencing customer care. We concentrated on skills and attitudes required by our staff and also found that company procedures and systems had an important effect on our staff's ability to support customers efficiently.

On Wednesday, we concentrated on enhancing customer relations and the need for creating a team approach throughout our company: the seamless organisation. We then discussed communication skills with particular emphasis on active listening and telephone techniques.

On Thursday, we homed in on complaints and how we can use them as a positive influence on customer perceptions. We learned to separate the immediate need for handling complaints from the more long-term benefit obtained from managing complaints. We then looked at ways of motivating our staff and how to use brainstorming techniques.

Yesterday we learned how to set standards for our various activities, how to measure them and why we need to feed back information on results to our staff. We examined a number of more widely used management tools to facilitate customer support and how some companies use these tools as sales aids.

Finally today, we examined how to put together the various elements we learned about during the earlier part of the week into a coherent customer care programme, including action and implementation plans. We accepted the need for internal selling and reviewed a way of doing this within our organisation. We came to the conclusion that customer care is a never ending activity and that we must therefore build on our past success to keep ahead of the game.

The thought I would like to leave you with is that everyone in the organisation must be actively involved in customer care:

Customer Care is not a spectator sport